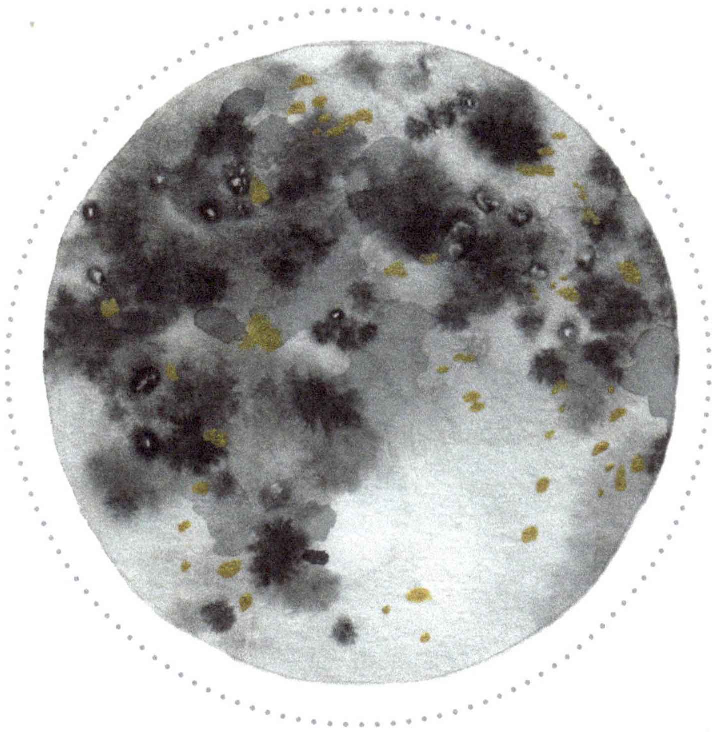

FriesenPress

Suite 300 - 990 Fort St
Victoria, BC, V8V 3K2
Canada

www.friesenpress.com

Copyright © 2021 by Rebecca Stanley
First Edition — 2021

www.rebeccastanley.ca

Illustrated by Jenni Haikonen
www.jennihaikonen.com

All rights reserved.

No part of this publication may be reproduced in any form, or by any means, electronic or mechanical, including photocopying, recording, or any information browsing, storage, or retrieval system, without permission in writing from FriesenPress.

ISBN
978-1-03-910505-8 (Hardcover)
978-1-03-910504-1 (Paperback)
978-1-03-910506-5 (eBook)

1. POETRY, SUBJECTS & THEMES

Distributed to the trade by The Ingram Book Company

Midlife Musings
Life, Love, God and the Universe

Rebecca Stanley

Dedicated to the stars that shine brightest in my sky

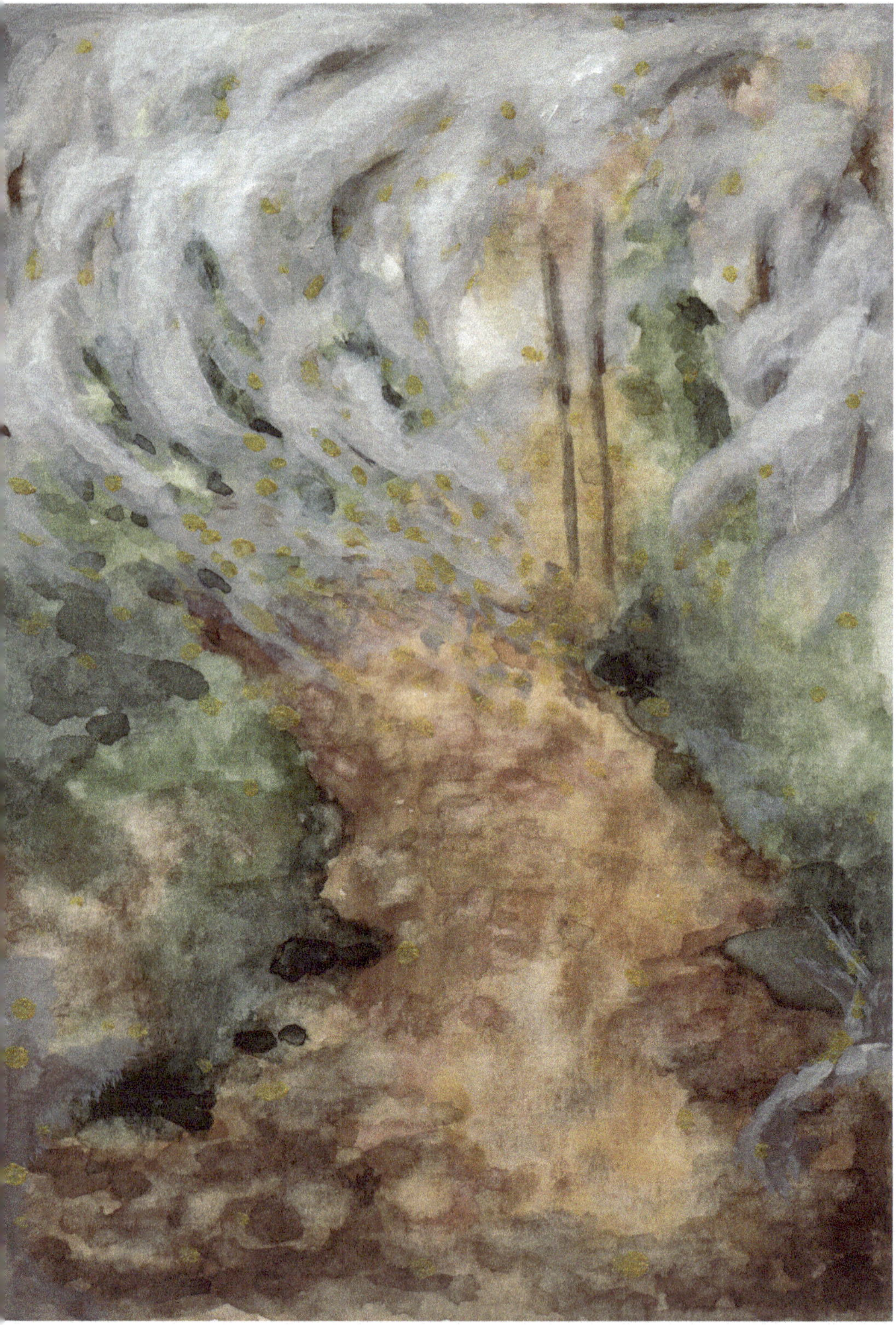

I

autumn

—

break and mend, break and mend

The first of my midlife poems struggled its way out of me as summer was turning to fall. A season of letting go, watching leaves fall to the ground and wither. Fresh crisp air mixed with death and decay. Such grief. Letting go is a tearing, a ripping, whether death; divorce; betrayal; loss of a friend, dream or job; or even the slow realization that the clock will not stop ticking, no matter how much we try to hold back time. Our culture needs better rituals, even simple acceptance of the time needed to grieve. Slow down. Do not be afraid. You are not alone.

Blood

Water

Stone

Cold

Here I sit

Broken yet fuller

Shadows

Illusion

Heart

Sick

Where are you now?

Yearning

Searing

Frozen

Tears

If only time was my friend

Instead of my captor

There is water in your blood

No warmth

No life

Stone

Cold

Why won't you come to my fire?

It is yours, my friend

It will warm your lifeless soul if you let it

Cut me and see

*I sit and watch
two spiders*

Tear each other limb from limb

Frozen, spellbound

Sorrowful

But if I intervene

My clumsy hands may slay them both

Instead I spy; I stare

I breathe to them

Stop

Will nature's instinct, holy grace

Step in to save these warring bodies

Whose self-inflicted cycle

Will be their end?

I hold my breath and wait…

A tear

A crack
A rip
No matter the word
The feeling's the same
Pressure in the chest
Lump in the throat
Aching in the bones
Chaos on the mind
Blurring of the eyes
The heart breaks

A tear small and undetected
A crack, gravity's next victim
A clean rip or jagged edge
No matter the damage
It leaves its mark
Despite the healing
Without warning
The pain resurfaces
As if time stood still

Good thing this heart of mine
Can break and mend, break and mend
Never quite the same but still pumping

Empty

Nothing but air

Not even reality

Anymore

I grasp

I try to hold on

But there is no point

Stars lost

Clouded over

Wind ceased

Even the lulling waves are no more

Until you see the whites in her eyes again

She does not exist

She never happened

It was only a dream

Runaway?

Where would I go?
There is no place without you
There is no wind without your breath
One day the world caves in and you are there
The next day the sun shines and you are there
A month from now
A year from now
Still you are there

You tear apart my heart
Then you mend it
You break my spirit
Then make it soar

Such power and yet none
I am a stone
That melts in your heat one day
And holds fast the next
Why must you dig my grave and yet
Call me to live?

Where can I go?
Without you I am lost
And yet with you I cannot find my way
I sink and swim and fly
Race across the mountains
And crash against the rocks
Each step I take is my last

Stop this turning
Twisting
Upside down
Just hold my hand
Look me in the eye
And remember who I am
Sit still
Just here
And be

Forgotten

How can that be?

A moment of wonder

A sense of freedom

A bond

Gone in a second

Something so precious

Tossed aside

As if it never existed

How can it be?

That we love

And walk away?

That we bond

And then break?

Is it inevitable?

Must that gift be lost

Thrown out

Or can we choose to honour what has been

To cling to what is

To preserve what is to come?

Not forgotten

Shadows

Dance and hide
Can never quite be caught
The shape of you
With no detail to cling to
Teasing memories
No flesh
No bone
No warm skin
Only whispers of reality

If the senses are no longer engaged
No smell upon the air
No sight of colours
Crevasses or cartoon grins
No sounds
No voices
No whispers to play back again and again
No taste of salt or sweet or sour
Nothing to touch but air

Then did we even exist
Or are we living in the shadowlands
Where spirits move undeterred
And human hands are no more

Show me you still exist
Reach out and swallow the shadow
That has overtaken you
Only then will we be free

Blood boils

Throat tightens
The rage inside threatens to erupt
Why does everyone else get to explode
Bubble over, throw F-bombs in the air
While I must squelch the fire
Hold back the tide
Like a cement dam built for appearance sake

He laughs at my pain
She jabs and cuts
He is indifferent after love poured out

Yet I must sit and smile
Pretend all is well
Cover the hurt
The disappointment
The tears
Or at least pretend the wound was only skin deep
When it actually pierced the heart
Left its mark

Don't tell me I am acting crazy
Say I need to get a grip
Don't pretend I don't exist
I am here
All of me
My pain
My rage
My tender heart

Tomorrow is a new day, yes
But now the dam stands taller
Not only holding back the flood
But also keeping out my deep well of love
It's your loss

Thrown out like trash

You pretend to still care
Say I matter
But your actions prove otherwise

How could I matter one moment and
Disappear the next?
Turned back
Silence
Worse even
Fake charity
Platitudes

Let's get coffee sometime
Don't say it if you don't mean it
My life used to be better with you in it
A mutual friendship made of clay
Give and take
But now all you do is take

Your absence steals my memories
Their authenticity
Questions whether our minds ever really met
Hands ever really clasped
Hearts ever really understood their winding paths

But I am not trash
It mattered
Souls did collide, my friend
Just thought we'd be left standing
Not forgotten
You cannot take back this mark you left
And one day
Perhaps
Our friendship will
Have meaning to you too
As you look in the mirror
And remember who you are

In the darkness

Reaching out

I thought you were there right beside me

But I feel nothing

Nothing but an icy chill

An empty breeze

A hollow where you used to lie

Devouring the stars with me

Where did you go, love?

Why are you so far away?

I see the shape of you

Yet no warmth

No signal of life

No connection between your soul and mine

Come back to me

Look me in the eye

Put away the distractions

Look beyond my flaws

Into my heart

That yearns to entwine

Become one

Body, soul and spirit

Am I invisible?
Is that the problem?
Perhaps all you see is a shadow
All you feel is a shell
An odd disfigured reflection
I am so much more, my love

If only we could reach out
Become entangled in life's swell
Feel alive once again
Desire, come visit
Breathe me in
Breathe me out
Uncover me
In the stillness
Touch me
Inside and out
In the darkness
Reach out
I am here

I hold you lightly

So as not to break you
To suffocate you
To scare you away
But will you stay?
Will you come close?
Or will you flee the moment I look away?
You are not mine
Yet you are a part of me
Your eyes
They see me
But does your heart?
I am yours forever
Captivated by who you are
Forever drawn to your tender heart
In awe of your spirit of life and love and peace
Mine forever
And yet I must let go
Trust your roots
They will hold fast
Now fly, my son
And let me marvel at the sight

I call out

And you do not answer
I reach out
You pull away
Echoes once bounced across the chasm
Now there is silence

I thought you would not disappear
In the night
In the morning
In the afternoon

You claimed me as yours
And then turned your back
Perhaps it was only a disguise
The smile
The sweet scent of mercy
The heavy cloak of comfort
Which you handed to me
Let me borrow
With an ocean of love in your eyes

Now I see I am left all alone
Words come cheap
Even from you
Am I ever on your mind?
Was I ever in your heart?

Or must I accept I was delusional
To think your grace would last even a moment
Past your desire?

Perhaps if I stand here long enough
You will return
And prepare a feast
Cover me with oil and light
Share sweet delights in exchange for favours
Not favours
Offerings
There is a difference

I offered them freely
One for each year
Expecting nothing in return
I hope you find such gifts elsewhere
If you decide not to return

I call out
Please answer

Is life a tragedy when seen in close-up but a comedy in long-shot?

Up close I see pain
Restlessness
Tears and sprains
Bruises and loneliness
Hatred
Grief
Desperation
Insanity
Greed
Friends turning their back
How is this anything but tragedy?

Is there comedy in this despair?
Will a smile cross your lips when the bitterness fades into the background?
Do I dare laugh in the face of today's chaos knowing tomorrow will bring light?

On Tuesday you were the bearer of bad news
Set on breaking my heart
Abandoned
Forgotten
But Friday is a different day

I will see you and laugh
Knowing the tears fall away and the joke is not on me
Smile
Life will go on

inspired by Charlie Chaplin

But Not Today

What is this feeling in the pit of my stomach?
Why do I wish the world would stop spinning
Let me sit by rushing water
Rock in a hammock
Kick my feet through crackling leaves
Each morning dawns another
Each night fades into black
Around and around we go
Never stopping

Please let me breathe
Let me sit on my bench and watch the sky
The chipmunks scurrying
Dogs bounding
Clouds drifting

Let me be, great dollar
That dictates my days
Sure, take a day off
But then pay the price

Great sadness, why are you on my doorstep today?
There is no time for us to chat
Or wallow
Or scheme

I cannot open the door when you knock
Yet you seep under the door uninvited

Perhaps tomorrow I will embrace your art
Sip from the cup of grief
Accept these feelings creeping and stirring within
But not today

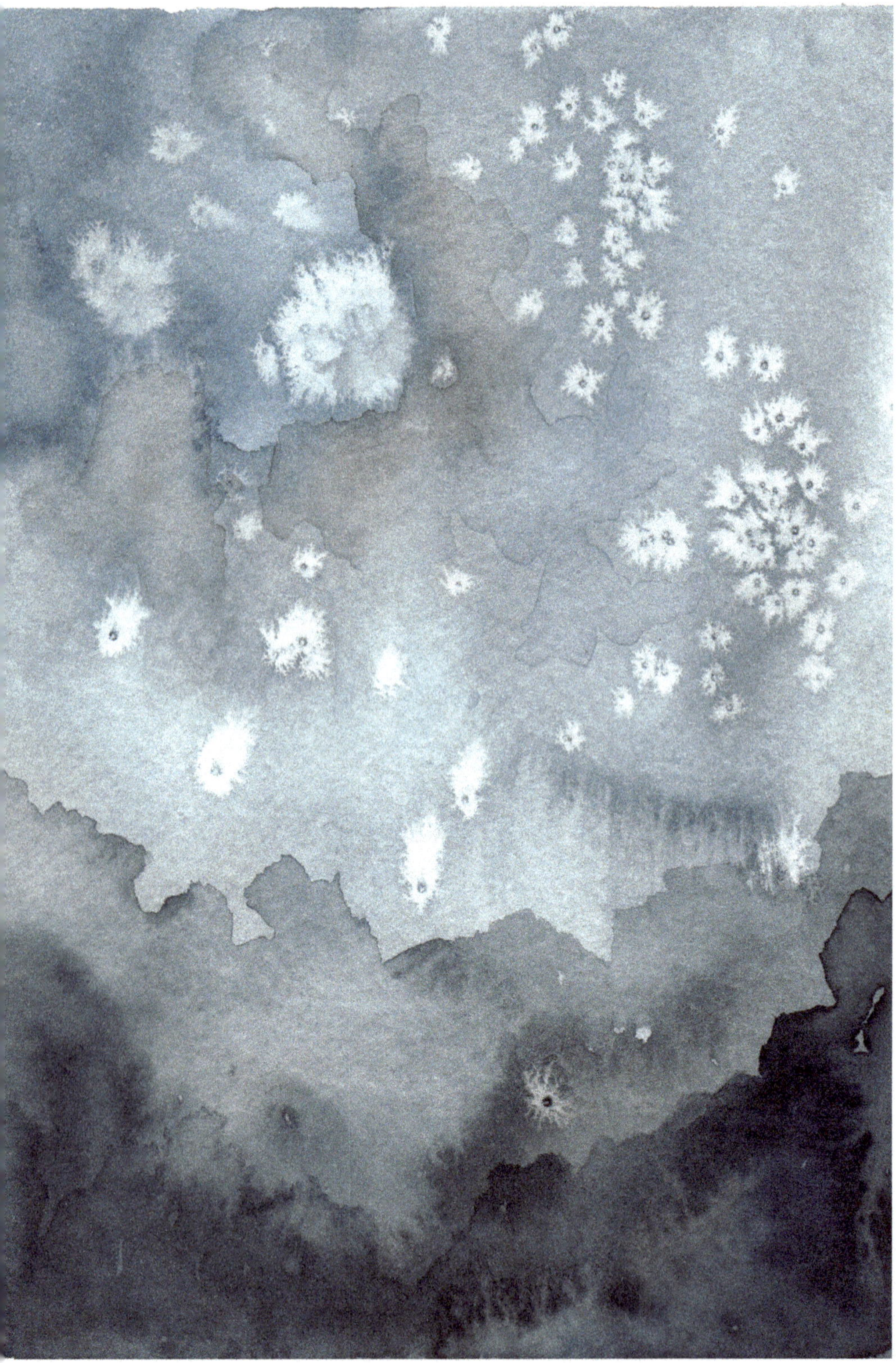

II

winter

—

fragile yet infinite

For many of us, midlife includes a "dark night of the soul," a bleak winter season in which the cold vastness of life is at the same time overwhelming and insufficient. Much of what we formally took for granted is now questioned and broken; it seems only to lead to hopeless desperation. And yet we must continue to live and eat and sleep and work and love those in our lives. We must dive into the deep where darkness abounds. We are invited to explore the vast silence of the universe. We may even be forced to walk alone on a frigid moonscape with no life in sight. But keep walking, my friend.

The great exploration

Into a space both familiar
And unknown
My soul
Both foreign and home
How do I describe this place?
Nooks and crannies seen by none
Hidden drawers
Trap doors
Mirrors
Fires
Flower petals
A sigh
A sob
Piercing light
Heavy darkness
Endless stars
One tiny snowflake
Fragile yet infinite

How do I describe a place
That contains the entire universe
While busting at the seams
With love for just one
Let alone all
That cross its path?

My soul is a thousand sunsets
Each river's song
You can enter in
And never find your way back
So much to explore
But will you make the journey?
Even dip your toe?
Or turn and walk away
From its blinding sun

Perhaps its moonlight is all you can handle
Dear friend
Where is your bravery now?
You will regret its unexplored vista
Such loss
Simply call and enter in
The invitation stands
The key already in your hand
The profound at your fingertips

Ever felt like a planet orbiting around the wrong sun?

The pull is irresistible
If you look up
You know you will be scorched
So with eyes to the ground you keep spinning
Spinning and spinning
Until up is down and down is up
Tossing and turning until all direction is lost

I must be in the right place
You reason
I feel warmth and light and calm resistance
All the while unaware
That searing talons reach towards you
Rays burn deep
Imprinting eternally
Leaving their mark
What can be done?
How do I loosen its grip?
If I let go
Will I tumble endlessly through the darkness
No tether
No saviour?

Or is there a place for me
A moment in time when all will align
Gravity will pull me towards my true destiny
My cosmic Home

Dead End

I walk the same path again
In my mind
In my heart
And I meet the same dead end
Why would it change?
With each step
I cross familiar sights
And sounds
And warning signs
Yet on I walk
I cannot stop myself
The path lures me
Beckons me
A beacon towards home

And yet the dead end remains
I cannot push my way through
I cannot imagine another end
Reality trumps illusion every time
Like Pavlov's dog I respond
Despite the insanity of it

I try again and again
Hoping the path will open up
To what, I don't know
But to something that calls me
In the depths of my soul
A piece of my heart will stand on this path
With the dead end in sight forever
I cannot abandon it
Even if I am seen by none
Blurred by moss
Weathered by storm
I will not go
The dead end is in itself beauty
Holding me captive to its chaos and art

Yet do I wish to die here?
There is no life
The whispering breeze of hope
More distant every day
Imagination does not sustain
Desire will not feed
The empty mirage buries the soul

At some point I must choose to abandon this path
Cease standing vigil at the dead end
Plant a monument
A headstone
And keep moving
My thirst will drive me forward
Eviscerated by isolation
I must find a different path
With life and growth springing forth

Take my hand
I cannot leave on my own
I cannot find my way
My eyes see only my beloved dead end
Show me the way
Move me
Call me
Love's sweet whisper

Am I Alive?

I must be
I feel your touch
I taste your skin
I must be alive
Because I smell your neck
And see your eyes
And hear your breath beside me

But when you disappear
Into the breeze
Abandon your post
Never to return
Will I cease to exist?
If I reach out
And find only empty space
Nothing to sink my teeth into
Nothing but burnt memories
And echoes of love's lullaby
Empty skies and barren seas
Will I find myself lost
No longer alive
The days unfolding without me
Suns rising and setting
While I watch from afar?
Or will these dry bones live again?

Twilight

Hits me like a cement door in the face
It no longer creeps in hardly noticed
Because now it rears up quickly
Its only purpose to remind me
That what was is no more
And what could have been will never be

Perhaps I was naive to think reality could have borne colour
Fluorescent and full of life
Light itself dancing upon my features
Its sweet touch tip toeing across my bare skin

I should have known it was too good to be true
That, instead, the grey of dusk envelops my being
The ghosts of fingers barely visible, but still felt
Piercing eyes looking right through me
While pretending to care

Why do my tears continue to fall
Mourning moments melted away
Never truly mine?

Gravestones mark the place I laid

Counting stars and secrets and Sunday sweets

Cut on thorns

Games gone

Laughter lost

Darkness teaches me my true name

Forever yours

Never yours

Only yours

How does it happen so fast?

Driving smoothly down the road

Not a cloud in sight

Without warning

They roll in

Take over the horizon

Causing chaos and darkness

Drowning out the sun

I try to push them back

Stuff them back in their place

But try as I might

We are surrounded

Swirling

Lifting us up into the eye of the storm

Why are we powerless to its pull?

Can we not see the dark horizon ahead

And avoid its path

Rather than drive straight into it?

Please

Next time

Can we take another road

And remain in the sun

With the top down

Music blaring
Smiles and crow's feet
Lazily holding hands

Next time
Please

New Year's Eve

With two hours left
Of this day
This month
This year
This decade
I look back and see
Pain
Love
Resilience
Hope
Despair
The mirror's reflection a source of
Wonder and terror

Who am I?
This mix of shadow and light
Chaos and art
Mind
Body
And Spirit
Blend to form a creature unknown to me
A stranger
Yet so familiar
Friend and enemy

Child and woman
Wise yet foolish

Good to finally meet you
I say to this beauty staring back
Wide-eyed and afraid
It is time to come out of the depths
Out from behind that wall built year upon year
Come out and play
Come out and be known
Come out to love and be loved

With two hours left
I look ahead and see
Sunrise after sunrise
Inviting life
Hope
Awakening
Breath upon breath
Offering peace and safety
Laughter
Singing
Thinking
Tears

Even heartache calls her out
Hand in hand
Summoning strength and affection
Silent glances speaking volumes
Fiery debates building understanding
Grief and sorrow
Passion and love
Walking beside and before
Sunset after sunset
Calling for reflection
Forgiveness
Mercy
Each a fresh start

With two hours left
I look up to the stars
Praying this next year
This coming decade
Will be gentle with her heart
So this scared child may run free

Feels like the world may end
Or it is stuck on repeat
Spinning
Turning
Reeling
No one knows when it will stop

So I stare at the same lights
From the same bench
Under the same stars
To remind myself that I remain

Here
Forever
Here
Never again

Breathe in the joy
Relive the sadness
Turmoil
Grace
Brokenness
Healing
Feel the sting so I know I am alive

Put on pause
Hidden away
But ever growing
Time does not stand still
It remains both friend and foe

Wind, remind me I am alive
Moon, my constant companion
Your stars a reminder of moments past
I will awake to a new day
Different and yet the same
Rays of light changing night to day
Taste and see all that is good
In this light I will remain

written during the COVID-19 lockdown

Some days

Clouds darken in the horizon

The calm waters begin to tremble

As I look out

I see darkness rolling towards me

Guessing only at its pace

The current comfort

Today's peace

Threatened

Bracing

What looms ahead will leave its mark

But other days

I am already in the storm

Lashing

Thrashing

Chaos

Turmoil

I cannot see

Above me

Below me

Around me

Yet in the distance

Light

That place of calm

I know it is out there

Not yet

But soon

And from its truth

I draw strength to get through

Can friendships end?

Are they simply for a reason
For a season
But not to endure?

Some are sown swiftly
Tossed together
Shallow and surreal
These don't last
Like a dandelion puff
Blown away in the wind

Some friendships are eaten by birds
Destroyed in the light of day
By wars or warts
Or worn down piles
Of broken promises
Jealousies
Betrayals
If forgiveness enters
It is too late

Some are forgotten
Neglected

Dried up in the heat
One usually scorched
The other oblivious to the heat
Or its damage

But some friendships are sown deep
Carried tenderly
Strong as a mighty oak
At the same time flexible
In the face of storms
The roots are deep
Understanding and love
Far from the shallows
Reaching into the universe
And pulling out treasures
Shared and surprising

These mighty friendships should not break
They are made of steel
And eclipse time

Or at least I thought they did
But perhaps all are finite
Broken

Soaked in blood from the start
And ashes in the end
Because they are human
Not saint

I am human
Not saint
Setting fire to friendships
Reaching out for treasure
And finding nothing but air
Between the stars
No matter how deep I think I go
The other does not care
Does not stand by me
I am alone
All must end

This I cannot accept
But cannot change
I am still yours

I could lie

And say I understand
Say I don't miss how it was
Tell you life is grand
All is well

Tell me what you want to hear
What will help you forget
Your part in this story?
Credit
Not blame
It's my gift to you

But let's be real
When the facade is broken
When I look in the mirror
The scars remain
The vice tightens
And I cannot be saved
From myself
Or from the shadow of who I was

But forget about this curse
It is not yours
You live in another world
Where flowers bloom again
And winter lifts

I will watch from behind a frosted glass
Admire your bravery
Covet your freedom
I will remember the days when I too
Ran in fields of gold

I could lie
And say I don't mind
Just don't forget I showed you those fields
They were mine
I will stand aside and take the blame
But give me some credit
When the sun shines again

You think too much
Of course I do
How else would I know
Forty scenarios
Each with its own ending
And choose the one I dreamed of

When I think
I see in colour
Not black and white
Words on a page
Faces and fingers
Furrowing eyebrows
I fuss and calibrate
Critique and question
Mulling things over
List upon list
Expectations
Calculations
My mind does not rest

You feel too little
Now that's not true
While my mind races
My heart palpitates
My stomach turns
My throat constricts

Lips dry not from thoughts
But feelings
I feel emotions I cannot name
I feel pain I cannot trace
I feel passion I cannot tame

You are wrong, my friend
For every thought there are a hundred feelings
You simply don't care enough to wait for me to figure them out
Much easier to assume I am cold and calculating
Better to be frozen out than burned, I suppose

But it's your loss
Each thought is a diamond
But each feeling a much rarer sapphire
Maybe an emerald
Or a ruby that soaks in the sunlight
And never lets it out

Here we are again
Face to face
This time will you mine for greater treasure
Or settle for yesterday's news?
Look me in the eye
Reach into my soul

Only there will you be touched
Perhaps even transformed

Don't get me wrong
My mind is an ocean worth exploring too
But you'll only dip your toes
Into who I am
Unless you discover
The sensations
Masquerading as knowledge
Peel back the layers
Don't miss out

Reality

Fantasy

Concrete

Abstract

Occurring

Imagined

Tactile

Ethereal

What is it about the fantasy that draws us in?
How can the imagined bring more satisfaction than the real?
Some experiences, the most profound searing ones
Combine the concrete and the abstract

You feel

You taste

You smell

You are touched

Heard

Seen

And yet it is a mirage

A fleeting dream

With no connection to the everyday

Being both real and imagined

Its superpower

Those moments
When you truly believe you could fly
You hear the drumbeat of courage
You taste success despite the odds
You feel a hand in yours
Providing warmth and love
But look down and see nothing there

Those moments
Of blissful connection
With a stranger who becomes your lifeline
For only a moment
A pair of eyes looks into your soul at a bus stop
And offers healing and peace for a fleeting blink
Before turning away

Those moments
Enraptured in a book or a movie that speaks into your life
As if the character walked right in the door
Those seasons you hold on to when someone knew you
Saw you
Loved you
But left you and is no more

Hold these moments, those seasons, tightly
There is magic in the meeting of two worlds
Transforming power in the melding
Of what is and what could be
Or what was
Or what is but cannot be seen
Gifts to be treasured
Despite the pain

The unspoken story

Expands and engulfs
Without warning
Without mercy
A snowball to the face
Out of nowhere
Knocking me off balance
If only for a moment
It is usually buried deep below the surface
Smothered by days and months passed
Hidden from sight
So when it pushes through
Ivy growing
Twisting
Not to be forgotten
It takes my breath away
Stops the heart
Fills the corners of the eyes
Tightens around the throat
Should I cut the vines down?
Stifle it once again?

Or accept it is here to stay
Wrapped around my heart
Some days a vice of grief and confusion
Others a warm blanket of comfort and acceptance
But forever a part of me

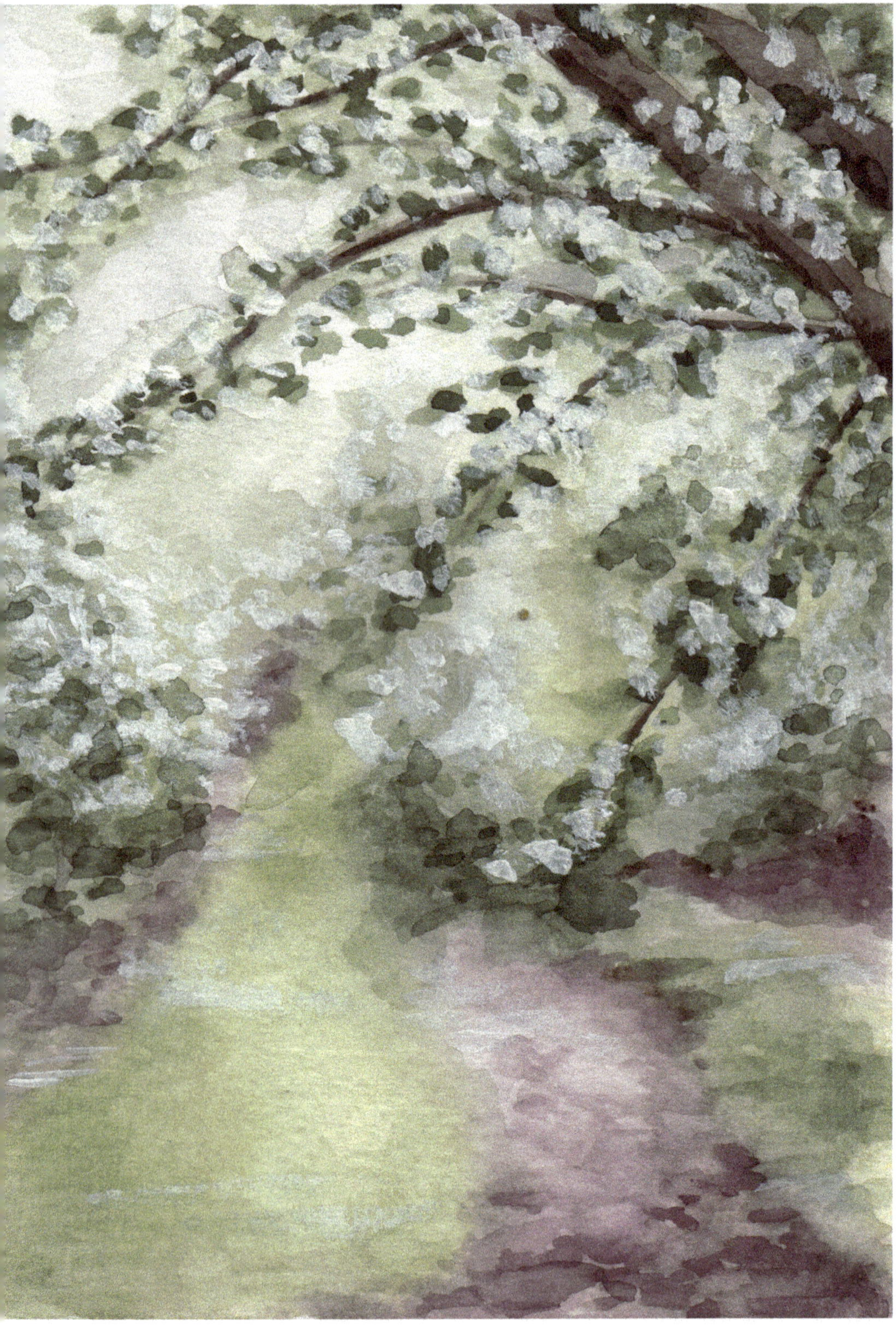

III

spring

—

the surge and swell of mending

No matter how long the winter, Spring does burst forth with new life. At times she surprises us; other times we watch her arrive, almost in slow motion. But Spring is not the synthetic perfection of plastic rows of buds synchronized in movement and display. She is, instead, a mixing of the dead of autumn now warmed by the sun's rays and ready to grow after the fallow of winter. The new life of Spring includes miscarriage and stillbirth. It is a slow awakening. It is new discoveries. It is planting and sowing and weeding and watering. A waiting for the tiny seed to grow.

Awake

Life all around

Springing forth

No longer deadened by the harsh cold of winter

Waking from its slumber

One sprig of purple

A carpet of green

Distant drumming

Whistling

Creaking

Chirping

A whisper

Then a soaring bird joins in

Calling for all to awaken and enjoy the sun's rays

Rushing wind

Or is it water?

Movement

Joyous awakening

By the kiss of the Creator

I am invited

Not to make it happen

To toil

Or even support

But to join the song

My own soul stirred to new life

Out of the winter's frost
Into spring's wondrous call

inspired by the vista and sounds above Rivendell Retreat Centre on Bowen Island, BC

Never been a great gardener

Letting one plant dry up and wither

Another drown in excessive care

One gets left in the dark

Another smothered in light and heat

Never took the time to learn what each needs to flourish

Never been a great gardener

Whether green thing or human thing

Never quite get the dosage right

This one I want to smother in love when he would rather keep distance

That one I neglect as she suffers in the dark

Another withers from my lack of affirmation

While still another drowns in a sea of expectations

But I want to learn

Speak to me, dear root

Let me learn from your seasons

Forgive my green thumb

As I plant and water

And restore

We'll get the dosage right, my loves

If your tears had words

What would they say?
Such a stirring question
So difficult to answer
Some days they would be screaming
Other days a mere whisper
Timid or a torrent
They speak a language I don't recognize
The tongues of angels
Foreign flames, founts unfolding
Today they grieve
Tomorrow they simmer in silence
Barely breathing
Yesterday they seethed
Feasting upon frustration

I must learn this new language
My tears have been present for decades
Yet I have not given them a voice
Tell me what you want, dear ones
Speak your mind
Enlighten my darkened understanding
Unmuted

Will you teach me
Of your miraculous powers?
Speak
I am listening

Silence beckons

Solitude sits on the doormat

Invite me in!

But what will we do, stranger?

You look boring to me

What if we don't get along?

You steal

You take

You move right in

And kick me out

What if you turn on me

An uninvited guest who will not leave?

Yes but what if instead

I show you treasures

Let you play

Take care of your chores

Give you space to breathe?

What if I have presents and candles

And chocolate and jewels

Tales of adventure

A feast of your favourite things?

I am not a stranger

I am yours

I stand at the door and knock
If you let me in
I will show you the universe

*written at the start of a 20 hour silent retreat

Dear Cove

Vast expanse of ocean

Mirrors my heart

My soul

Limitless and daunting

Teeming with the unknown

Darkness, beauty

Splashes of light and air

Stumbled upon a cove

Hidden from sight

Alcove of treasures

Calm delight

Alluring

Inviting

Healing

A refuge

My sanctuary

This haven has drawn me deep

In peaceful waters

Facing fears in a safety net

Of sinew and tenderness

Shielded from terrors in the deep

Ushering in rising dawns
Warming my skin and bones

But this cavern has its own shadows
Murkiness at twilight
Silence when I ache for connection
Blurring
Tangling
Stirring up
As I wrestle
With even an inch of disclosure
Of revelation

Am I actually alone even here in this nook
I thought contained new life and asylum?
Was it illusion
Fantasy
A fool's paradise?

I should see it for what it is
Simply another piece of dirt
Imagined riches
Endless grains of sand washed up
Against rock and quarry
Brackish waters

Lulling me into
A sense of security and home

But this fractured corner is so much more
It is the place I found the courage to tip toe off the shores
It is wonder
Countless stars above
The rhythm of cresting soothing waves
The surge and swell of mending
The soft touch of discovery
The taste of freedom

I cannot stay here
I must venture out
Traverse and hunt and burrow
Dive into the shadows of the briny deep
Explore the scope of these seas

But tell me, dear cove
Sanctuary of light and love
Can I find you again?
Will you welcome me in?
Your waters will change
No sky remains intact

But can I return to wade my tired feet
In the pool that met me in fear
And transformed this stony heart?

Can I kiss each grain of sand
In gratefulness and joy for who I have become?
If I burst with stories of adventure and raiders upon the high seas
Will you smile and share your own tales
Of sightings
Of life and death
And the in between?
Leave space, dear cove,
For my feet to once again
Imprint upon your sands
I will return

*this one wrestled itself out during a day alone in a cabin
on the ocean in Qualicum Beach, BC*

Finger's Stroke

The soft touch of the lower lip

A tracing of the spine

Sweet caress

Tongue's bliss

Heaving

Swaying

A rhythm all our own

Who needs a map

When you are invited to explore

Those favourite spots

The lightest brush

Starts at the hidden crest of the neck

Tracing downward

Ripe and rising

Electrified by finger's stroke

Melting

Molting

Misting

Waters turning

Tossing

Adventurer

Have you found your treasure?

Can you taste it?

See it gleam?

Pleasure's power
Resting in the steamy in-between
Anticipation building
As rocks are overturned
Crevasses cut
Every inch explored
Until life gasps
Rising forth out of the writhing
It breaks free
With one heave
Or two
Peace washes over
Both the raw and the quivering
Until next time, Traveller
Sleep well
You'll need your strength

To the Centre

Why is the Centre so hard to reach?
It is the promised destination
I journey
Following each stone placed before me
Moving inward
Towards the Centre
Yet suddenly the stones veer left
Then right
A straightaway
Anticipation builds
As I weave closer to the Centre

Yet they turn outward
And after a leg of my journey
I am now on the outer edge
As far from the Centre as possible
Despite all my effort

I meander closer
At times on the long stretches
I pick up my pace
Even dare to look up from my feet
From the stones that lead the way
Aware of my surroundings for but a moment

Wait

This path looks exactly like where I started from

What wasted steps

Wasted time

But no

It is only an illusion of trust

Keep going, my friend

I walk the journey alone

Trusting the Voice that whispers

This is the way

Trust me

In a moment

Almost by surprise

I am at the gate of the Centre

White stones invite me in

Even here there are chambers to visit

The Centre calls me in

But even here I must search

Explore

Trust

In each room a white stone grounds me

Until finally I am ready to stand on the Centre

Eyes closed
Invited in
The rushing wind
Behind my eyes
A portal calling me deeper
Apart from creation and yet part of it
Into the Centre
Still tied to the labyrinth of my days
The journey part of the destination

*inspired by the Labyrinth at Rivendell on Bowen Island, BC

Drop, Stone

Stone

Drops

Sinks down slow

Past the rushing waters

Fish

Fermenting flow

Tumble of twig and

Tearing of time

Lands softly below the tumult

Exists in a space all its own

Where soul stands still

Calmness creates

The weight of wisdom holds firm

On the surface

One fights against the current

Exhausted

Beaten down

Another's caught by the swirling

Frantically flailing

Seeking relief

Another sits at river's edge

Afraid to enter

Without being swallowed up
Glorious River
Bubbling with life
Teach me to sink down deep
Even as life rushes by
Sink down slow
Drop, Stone

Wake up

Take a shower
Brush my teeth
No
First eat breakfast
Feed the dogs
Check the news feeds
Scroll for connection
Then brush my teeth
And off to work

A rhythm built on hollow sounds
Anemic
Nourishing nothing but the body
These precious moments
Before the pressures and chores of life step in
Could feed me
Draw me deeper

Take a deep breath
Smell the sunflowers in the kitchen's rays
Or the sour neck of the panting puppy
Eager to greet with affection and love
Ignore the phone
Instead

Soak in your belovedness
Recall words of hope
Of acceptance
Of joy
Plan an adventure
Think of happy memories
Take a moment to share a laugh with a friend
Find a beetle
Maybe a ladybug
And set it free

Savour
Sit
Soak
Speak
Simple acts of delight
To fill the soul
As the day begins
A rhythm pressing deep within
Good morning, world!

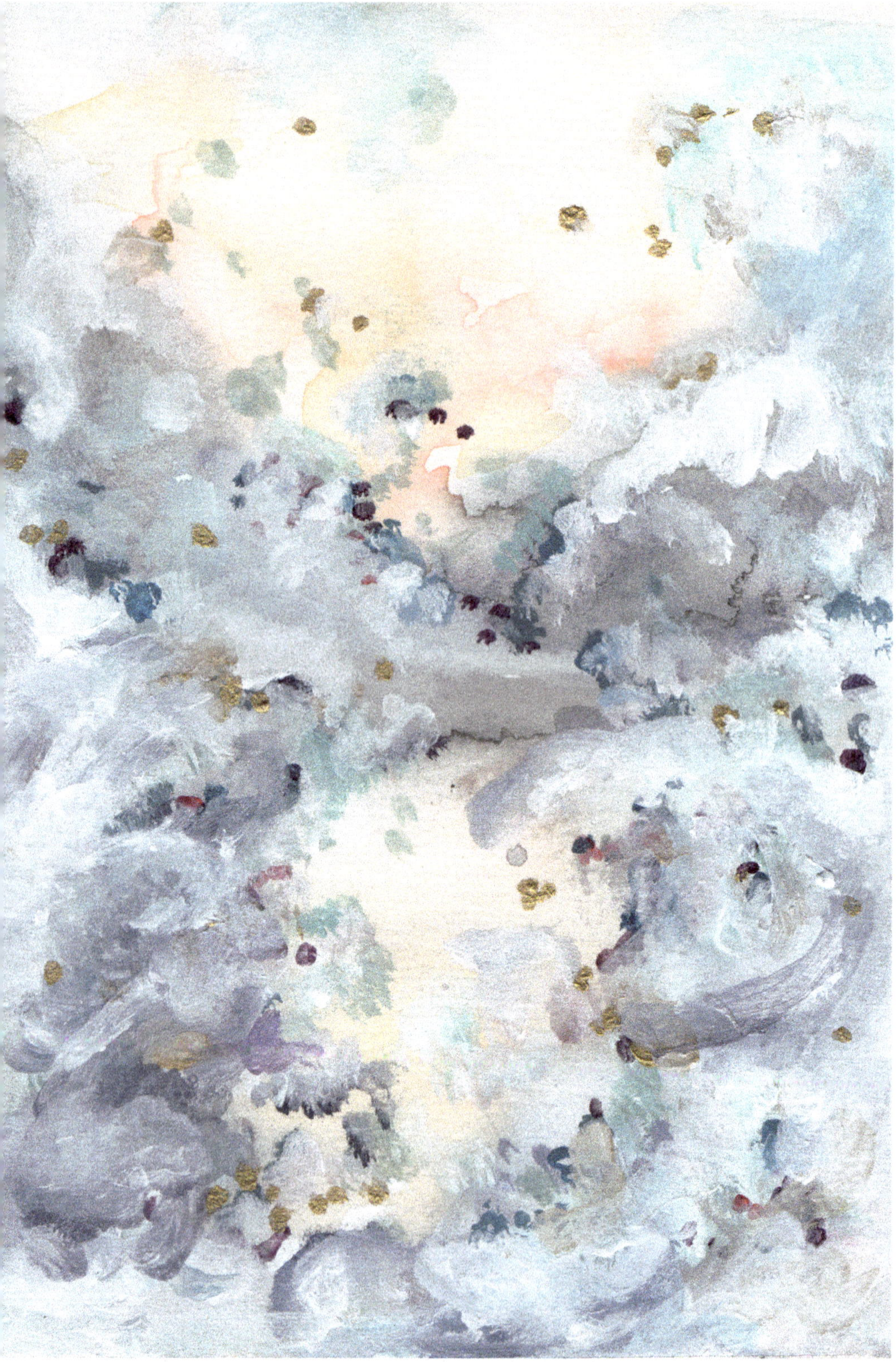

IV

summer

—

swallowing the stars

There is a part of me that hates summer. I am pale and freckled. I burn easily. But despite the heat, summer is a time to slow down and enjoy our world, enjoy one another. It is a season of being, not doing. Swaying in a hammock. Skinny dipping in a lake. Watching the dancing flames of a fire. Simply listening to the night sounds. And best of all, gazing at the stars. Summer reminds us we are alive and young and worthy. It is the memories of youthful summer nights; first kisses; the lingering touch that both electrifies and soothes; the night's breeze on bare skin. In the summer of midlife, I learn to love myself - my body, my mind, my feelings. Acceptance and freedom are splashes of cold water refreshing the soul on a balmy day.

Nobody's watching

No one really knows
Shadows cast in blue
Grey upon my door
Anything could happen
Vases break
Ice melts away
Hearts implode
You remain unshaken
Oblivious behind your sheltered screen
Unaware of tremor
Chasm
Hidden hollow
Searing pain lost upon unfazed flesh

Since nobody's watching
Why not throw off this wrenching
Whispering mind
Flashback to sweeter times
Throw off the weight of sorrow or misgiving
Strip down to only skin
Which senses every brush
Crash and kiss
Tastes each layer of delight
Air breathed deep into the lungs

You will miss it all, my sweet
If you don't look up
Even for a moment
To gaze upon my naked genius
Able to mend and break in concert

Perhaps one day you will meet me on the bank
And care to ask how I rose again
While nobody watched

But for now I am content
In knowing my shadow is my ally
This cleft a healing place
I stand and sing and dance and cry
And laugh while nobody watches

*One wraps around you like
a well-fit glove*

Comfortable and warm

A sigh of relief

Another grips you tight

Laced in fear and desperation

Breath held

Yet another lightly enters your space

Timid and fragile

Anticipating

This one jumps on you

Vibrant and carefree

Loosening a smile without effort

That one breathed you in deep

Savouring the moment that may be consigned to memory alone

Still another falls upon you

Limp and yearning

Never admitting its need

Finally another clinging for dear life

Wretched and heaving

Pulling you down as you stand under its anchoring weight

The last safely landing

Knowing

Seeing

Caressing

Giving as much as it takes
Each embrace a melody
Some etched deep
Ringing in your ears
Quivering long past its touch
Some forgotten in the shadows
Yet all imprinting Love

That's messed up!

Words of judgment
Seeping with lack of understanding
Spoken at a distance
Blind eyes assuming sight
Try walking in my shoes
Take a peek at my soul
If you dare
And you will find meaning in what you call mess
Art in the chaos
Understanding that what you call messed up
Brings light and love and life
It holds darkness, yes
And the grey dances alongside the colours
If you took the time to know me
To listen
To really see
You would not be so quick to judge
Because one day you will be where I stand
The black and white faded to grey
The acceptable no longer enough
One day you will be surprised by blessings they label a curse
An unexpected gift that leads you back to the path, dear lost one
Or helps you uncover a new one, sweet sojourner

Judge all you want
But one day, young one,
You will wake up and know your story is also a beautiful mess
And you'll love it

Your love

Your spirit

It is only a trickle right now

I hear it

I am reminded of its cool refreshing

But what I see is scarce

Not the abundance you have promised

The earth has dried up

The sun is scorching

Pools are shallow

The river is but a brook

And I can see its end

But the trickling sounds

Remind me it is still living

And moving

And mine for the taking

Refreshing my soul

Renewing my mind

The gentle breeze cools

I share this living water

With the earth

Its creatures

And it does not end

It bubbles forth once again

Mirror, mirror on the wall,
Who is the fairest of them all?
Freckle-faced wide-eyed shadow with the impish grin?
Sister-mama playing house with dear baby blond?
Teacher of teddy bears and dolls from across the sea
Play acting her dream of countries afar?

How about the one ashamed of all but her mind
Covering arms and shoulders
Pimples and heart's desires?
Do you choose the one tainted by first love?
Or she who blossomed in the womb of friendship and grace found?
What about the make-up-less tanned beloved
Discovering treasures in desert and garden afar?

It must be the warrior
Birthing with all her might
Tearing and pushing
Creating three glorious sights
There is always the timid baby fat-laden neighbour
Losing herself in sleepless nights and daily labour
She rose for those moments of gasping delight
When child and mother re-coupled,
Eye to eye
Skin to skin
Laugh to laugh
Love to love

What about she who
Wing clipped
Flapped against the cage
Raising dust and feces upon all in her wake?
Could it be she
The waffling wife
Pushing and pulling
Scared of exposing her life?

It must be the one finding joy
Pouring out
Not the one in the shadows
Broken glass
Tear stained mouth
I see her standing cap and gown
Bouquet at her side
Family beaming with pride
Despite the uneasy ride

This one
She hides
That one
She flies
Over here she is naked
Desire in her eyes

But what about her?
The one aging in slow-motion
While the world spins madly
Causing a commotion

Peel it back
Each layer
If she allows
Take a glimpse
Touch and wonder
Is it flesh and bone?

Mirror, mirror
Endless mirror
Lost in time
She is a marvel
This woman of mine!

Mirror, mirror on the wall,
Who is the fairest of them all?
Each freckle a kiss
Each blemish a wish
Marred only by self-doubt and lost vision

O Fair One
Come home
Peel back your skins and
Delight in each angle
Each one a curious spectacle
Love's Way
Love's Gift

When I look into your eyes

I see the day I finally met you
Understood you are made of glass
And flesh and stone and spirit
You are not kind
And yet you are
You are not strong
Yet you are the strongest I have known
You turn in circles
But you seem to know the way

What would you think if I told you
You will never be alone
But you will stand solitary
Not to be understood
One day you will close those beautiful eyes
And see for the first time
What you thought was yours
Will be lost
And in its place
The universe

Don't leave me yet
There is so much more to say

Not even one word will cross my lips
For you already know them all
Whispers of wine and wool and willow
Pieces of precious plastic pride
Follow me
I promise not to lose my way again

Where would you go if not with me?
Why signal someone else when I am right here?
I hear your song brushing my neck
Your hopeful tune carrying me forward
We are alive, you know
Never going back
But somehow ever repeating
The rhythm and rhyme of you

I am free
I am imprisoned
I am old
I am reborn
My own
But only yours

Look again
We are still here
Forever gone

In a house

In the woods

I met a man

Full beard

Smiling eyes

Told me he lived off the land

Knew nothing of technology

Beyond the chair he sat on

And the fire he ate from

Yet he was content

As long as the spiders kept spinning their webs

The birds kept singing their tunes

And the wind visited every second day

What do you do

I asked

Don't you get lonely?

How do you fill your days?

He simply chuckled

Looked me straight in the eye

And said

I've been waiting for you!

Preparing the food

Lighting the candles

Making a blanket to keep you warm

Now sit
I have so many stories to tell you
My Beloved
And we talked all night until the sun rose again

Here I sit

Undone

Heart beating fast

Please don't leave

I need you

To see me

And smile

To hear me

And understand

To breathe me in

Not let go

Ok I don't need you

And you don't need me

But stay close anyways

You are light

Freedom

Mystery

Eternal hope

In a barren wasteland

I cannot recall your name

You are a stranger now

But split me open

And your light will escape

From its hidden corner
It has a life of its own

Even if forgotten
On this side of reality
Exposed to my heart alone
It has life
No
It is life
Faded or bright
It leads me forward
This little light of mine

Flesh

Shivers in the breeze
Shimmers in the moonlight
Eyes
Caught in a gaze
Unexplainable
Tongues
Speak the language of angels
Whispering secrets caught in the wind

A laugh breaks free
Questions abound
Yet caution is lost
For just a moment
Time stands still
And the earth breathes one breath
In and out
Caught up
Full

Hands
Press together
Feet
Intertwine

A collective
Creation
At its best
Where life meets life
And is forever changed

Shedding skin

She dances in the moonlight
The soft cresting of waves
Her rhythm
The surge and swell of mending
Sand beneath her feet
Melting away
Warmth caressing her skin
Alive and electric
While the evening breeze wisps her hair
Feathers of a soaring bird

Twirling
Spinning
Laughing
Loving
Face to the sky
Swallowing the stars

She sheds her skin
In a moment both free and exposed
Naked
As she once was
Before her skin grew layer upon layer

Human fabric trapping
Hiding
Suffocating

Tonight she smiles
Unaware of the discarded shell
Dead cells at her feet
Allowing her to breathe anew
All around the taste of freedom
She dances in the moonlight

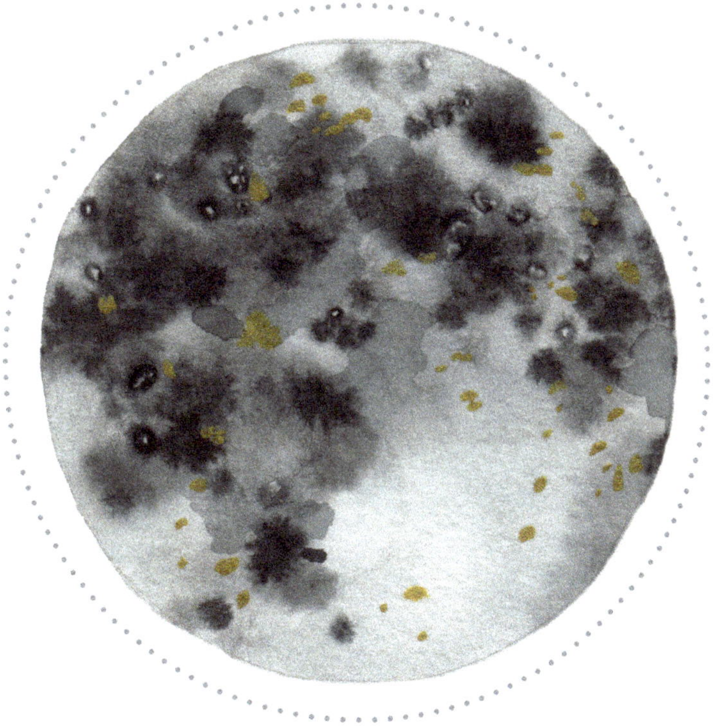

CPSIA information can be obtained
at www.ICGtesting.com
Printed in the USA
BVHW061505120521
607086BV00001B/3

9 781039 105041